D1203471

# MING DYNASTY CHINA

Bonnie
Hinman

PURPLE TOAD
PUBLISHING

P.O. Box 631
Kennett Square, Pennsylvania 19348
www.purpletoadpublishing.com

### ANCIENT EGYPT
### MEDIEVAL ENGLAND
### MING DYNASTY CHINA
### RENAISSANCE ITALY
### THE SPANISH EMPIRE

**PUBLISHER'S NOTE:** The data in this book has been researched in depth, and to the best of our knowledge is factual. Although every measure is taken to give an accurate account, Purple Toad Publishing makes no warranty of the accuracy of the information and is not liable for damages caused by inaccuracies.

**ABOUT THE AUTHOR:**
Bonnie Hinman has written more than 30 books for children including an award-winning biography on W.E.B Du Bois, which was listed on New York Public Library Books For the Teen Age in 2006. She lives in Southwest Missouri with her husband, Bill, and near her children and grandchildren.

Printing   1   2   3   4   5   6   7   8   9

Publisher's Cataloging-in-Publication Data
Hinman, Bonnie
   Ming Dynasty / Bonnie Hinman
      p. cm. — (That's me in history)
Includes bibliographic references and index.
ISBN: 978-1-62469-046-4 (library bound)
1. China—Civilization—960-1644—Juvenile literature.
I. Title.
   DS750.72 2013
   951.026—dc23
                                                        2013936507

eBook ISBN: 9781624690471

Printed by Lake Book Manufacturing, Chicago, IL

# CONTENTS

# CHAPTER 1
# Welcome to Peking

I'm so glad you're here! I've been waiting by the inner city gate since daybreak when the ceremony started. We'll miss the procession if we don't hurry. It started at the Gate of Greater Brilliance. The Son of Heaven (our emperor) and his officials and army officers are leading the way. Usually Emperor Wanli stays in his palace in the Forbidden City. When he does travel through the streets of Peking, the shops close and we all have to stay inside our houses. But today is special. The Son of Heaven is leading the procession to the Altar of Heaven where he will pray for rain. Everyone can watch this time—that's why the streets are so crowded.

The drought this year—1585—has been terrible. The farms outside the city have had almost no rain since last year. Now that it's May, rain must come or there will be no food. My father is a government official, so

Emperor Wanli sometimes used Elephants to pull his carriage when visiting the Altar of Heaven.

Wanli became emperor of the Ming Empire at nine years old. He was assisted by statesman Zhang Juzheng until he turned 19. Juzheng was a good administrator and directed many improvements in the Chinese government systems.

my family won't starve, but many peasants will have nothing to eat and will die. Father told me that the emperor is responsible for making sure that the peasants have food. That's why he is making this four-mile trip to pray at the open-air altar that his grandfather built in 1530. My father says that the gods might pay more attention if the emperor allows the people of the city to watch. Even so, we have to be careful. The police might decide to chase young boys away no matter what the emperor says.

Father thinks it will be hard for the emperor to make this long walk on foot rather than in his sedan chair. He is only twenty-two years old and is not used to walking so far. He has spent most of his life in the palace. Emperor Wanli wanted to walk this time and wanted all his officials and soldiers to walk as well. Look—we can watch from this stairway where we can't be seen.

Here they come! Everyone is wearing matching blue robes, even the military men. I don't hear any music, but their feet are loud as they march. Do you see any robes trimmed in gold or jade? That would be a clue as to which man is the emperor. Over there are the government officials where my father must be marching. On this side are the army officers. I think there are supposed to be 2,000 men in each group. Look—can you see my

**Ming dynasty military attire**

father? He seems as serious as the rest of the marchers. The emperor must have passed by now—and he must have been dressed like everyone else, because I didn't see any special clothing.[1]

Come on; let's go to the Altar of Heaven. Maybe we can see him there. I know a short cut. Did I tell you that my name is Liu Chi? I'm named after an honorable ancestor who was a great scholar. Chinese boys are often named after ancestors. I am ten years old and hope to be a great scholar myself when I finish my education.[2]

*Boy Riding a Goat*, fifteenth-century scroll painting by Lü Wenying

The Altar of Heaven, later called the Temple of Heaven, was built between 1406 and 1420 in southern Peking. It is now a UNESCO World Heritage Site, which is a title given to historically important buildings all over the world.

Over there is the Altar of Heaven, and here comes the procession. Climb up here on this stone wall, and we'll see if we can tell which person is the emperor.

That has to be him. He's the one who is kowtowing on the terrace while the others are lining up outside the wall. Father said the emperor will give a speech to the most important officials, who will gather in a tent beside the altar.

The ceremony will take a long time, and it's very hot out here. Let's go back to my house so I can show you where I live. Perhaps my mother will give us a copper coin so we can buy a drink at the market. Then I will show you more of our city.[3]

# THE MONGOL HORDE

The Mongols were a nomadic people well-known for their fighting skills.[4] Genghis Khan, the first great Mongolian ruler, and his descendants conquered much of the known world beginning in the early 1200s. The Mongol Empire eventually stretched from the Pacific Ocean on the east to Eastern Europe on the west, and then to Russia and much of the Middle East.

Genghis Khan's grandson, Kublai Khan, conquered all of China after a long struggle. He founded the Yuan Dynasty, which was both an official Chinese dynasty and a part of the Mongol Empire. The Yuan Dynasty was officially established in 1279 when Kublai Khan defeated the last holdouts of the Song Dynasty in Southern China. He reigned until 1294.

Kublai Khan stabilized China and made it a military power. The Mongols kept most of the administrative structure of the Song Dynasty, but replaced all of its officials with Mongols or other non-Chinese people.[5]

The Chinese resented this. They were also unhappy that the Mongols placed little importance on education. While the Mongols did leave a legacy in China, the Chinese never considered them more than barbarian invaders.[6]

Natural disasters, famines, and plagues did not help the Yuan cause, and the later Yuan emperors became less interested in

Mongol warriors at the battle of Kalka River

governing the country. When rebels approached in 1368, Toghan Temür, the last Yuan emperor, fled the capital city of Dadu (which is now Beijing). The Mongol Empire persisted, but it no longer controlled China. The country passed into the Ming Dynasty.

# CHAPTER 2
# My Home in the *Hutong*

Welcome to my *hutong*. That's what we call our neighborhoods. Several of our homes are joined together and divided by narrow streets, which are also called *hutong*. There are several hundred *hutong* in our city. Since we Chinese like to make our houses face south, most of the *hutong* run east and west. There are smaller paths that go north and south in our neighborhoods so that we can go places more easily.

This is the front door of my *siheyuan*, or house, right here. It's a courtyard house, which is the kind of house that most families live in. Go through the door and into our outer room, and I'll show you what I mean. All of the rooms are built in a square or rectangle around an open courtyard in the center. In our courtyard we have a beautiful garden with benches and a fish pond. Homes for poorer people are smaller, but each still has a tiny

Model of a courtyard *siheyuan*

courtyard. High government officials and princes live closest to the Forbidden City. Their houses have several courtyards and many more rooms than we have.[1]

This is our courtyard. The old woman who is sitting in the shade is my grandmother. She lives with us, as do my older brother and his wife. Let's bow to my grandmother and say hello, and then I will show you the rest of our home. Her eyes are weak, but she sees us. She sits out here often while working on her embroidery.

My room is across the courtyard. Did you notice that my grandmother sits with her feet on a small stool? She can no longer walk because her feet were bound from the time she was six years old until she was almost ten years old. It is a custom to wrap a girl's feet tightly so that they won't grow too large. Tiny feet are considered beautiful in China, and it's harder for a woman to get a husband if her feet have not been bound. It is a painful process.

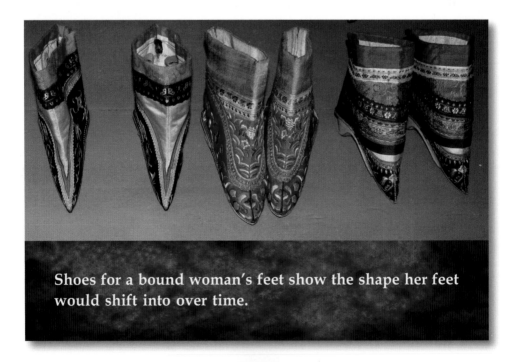

Shoes for a bound woman's feet show the shape her feet would shift into over time.

Some girls die from infections caused by the wraps, and most are no longer able to walk except with small steps.[2]

My mother's feet were never bound because my grandmother refused to allow her only daughter to have that done to her. It was good fortune when my father didn't care whether his wife had bound feet. My little sisters run freely because Father says it's a cruel and unnecessary custom. He says that he'll find husbands for my sisters when it is time, and the men will be happy to have such hardworking and beautiful wives, tiny feet or not.

Here is the room where I sleep with my two younger brothers. That raised platform is called a *kang*. In the winter, heat from the stove comes through vents under the *kang* and keeps the area warm. We sleep on the *kang* on mats. Our little sisters sleep in our parents' room on their *kang*, and my older brother and his wife have their own room with a *kang*. Grandmother has a small room to herself.[3]

Our servants cook for us in their quarters near

A *kang* with a *kang* table for refreshments placed atop

the front door. Sometimes Mother helps because she likes to cook. There is a big stove and some shelves, but not much else in the room for preparing food. We eat our meals in many different places. In the summer we sit in the courtyard, and in the coldest parts of winter, we may eat while sitting on our *kang*.

The carved wooden piece of furniture in the next room is our ancestor altar. It looks a little like a tall desk. It is decorated with drawings of some of our ancestors. We come in front of the altar to pray and to honor them. Sometimes we leave gifts of food and incense there. In China we believe that our ancestors are still part of our families even if they have died. It is important to remember them.[4]

Ming-style altar table used for placing pictures and objects of family members from the past.

An abacus is a counting device that was used in Asia and Europe for over 2,000 years. An accomplished abacus user can add, subtract, multiply, divide, and calculate square and cube root values just by moving the beads in certain ways.

Let's ask my mother for some copper coins to spend at the market. She'll be happy that we have been honored by a visit from you. She's probably sitting at a table on the other side of the courtyard working on the household accounts. My mother can read and write, unlike most other Chinese women. Almost all Chinese men believe that women don't need to learn to read and write or use the abacus. My father doesn't believe that and taught my mother when they were first married. He says that she can use the abacus for math faster than he can.

Mother is generous and gives me several coppers to spend at the market. Let's go out the back door and run down the small path to a *hutong* where there are shops. We could buy some noodles at the shop and some tea to drink. No, wait; let's buy candied fruit and maybe a sesame cake. Hurry up. I'm so hungry. After we eat, we'll see the Forbidden City.

# DINNER WITH THE EMPEROR

Few people of the Ming Dynasty were ever invited to dinner in the Forbidden City, but if you had been one of those lucky people in the early 1600s, this is what it might have been like.

You would enter the Forbidden City at the Meridian Gate, which is on the south side of the huge complex. Once inside, you would walk across a courtyard and over the Golden Water Bridge. Another vast courtyard would bring you to the Gate of Supreme Harmony, but you wouldn't be in the banquet hall yet.

Next is the Hall of Supreme Harmony, which is at the top of many steps. By now you may wish that you were riding in a sedan chair like the emperor does. The Hall of Middle Harmony is next, and finally you would reach your destination, the Hall of Preserving Harmony. Banquets and government examinations are held here.

The first thing you notice is the music of a *haiao,* which looks like a bamboo flute. The music is unlike any you have heard before—it is very beautiful and peaceful. You hear other instruments but can't identify them. The sounds blend in a way that makes you feel happy.[5]

There are many people in the room, and all are dressed in brightly colored tunics with elaborate embroidery. There is only one woman, and she must be the empress. She is dressed the fanciest of all. She wears a shiny pink tunic with embroidered scenes, and beads sparkle among the stitches. A short cape drapes over her shoulders.[6]

At last the emperor enters and all of the guests kowtow to him. He waves for everyone to stand and then be seated. Finally there will be food.

The emperor and his wife eat off pure gold dinnerware as a symbol of their importance. The rest of us use the famous white porcelain

Hall of Preserving Harmony

plates painted with blue designs. There are many vases, cups, and jars painted in the same way.[7]

The food arrives at last. The Chinese have valued a healthy diet since ancient days and believe that food and medicine are often the same. You will be served soup and several varieties of fruit and vegetables. The Chinese believe that the soup must have a certain proportion of water to other ingredients to be nutritionally complete.[8]

There are several main dishes to sample. You may have stir-fried sheep tripe, which is sheep stomach. Perhaps you will eat pickled trotters, which are pig's feet and heads. There might be deep-fried sparrows and sea cucumbers. All the dishes have rich sauces or broth. There will be lots of tea, and there might be candied fruit to finish the meal.[9]

After dinner there is entertainment by some of the imperial eunuchs. The eunuchs wear face paint, and some are dressed as women. They perform an old legend that makes the emperor bend over laughing.

At last the emperor rises from his chair and leaves the hall. This is a signal that everyone else must leave as well. It's a long way back to the Meridian Gate where your transportation will be waiting. The exercise is welcome after such a feast.

# CHAPTER 3
# The Forbidden City

This is the sweets shop. What kind of candied fruit do you want? They have apricot, lychee, apple, green plum, haw, and many others. The candy maker boils fruit pieces in water with crushed rock sugar and then lets it dry. Or maybe you'd like to try a bobotang? It's made of maltose and glutinous rice and almost melts in your mouth. I also like sesame seed candy. There are so many kinds, and I like them all. Today I think I will have some candied apricot. You might like it, too.

We'd better get going. We can eat our sweets as we walk. The Imperial City covers about three square miles (eight square kilometers) in the middle of Peking. The Forbidden City is in the middle of the Imperial City. The most important government officials and generals live

The Forbidden City

The Forbidden City
front gate

nearest the Imperial City. Less important officials live farther out in a circle. Poorer people live even farther from the center. I live in the middle of the circle of less important officials. Father is a government official, but he isn't one of the most important ones yet.[1]

No person may enter the Forbidden City unless the emperor asks him to visit. His family and staff live there with him in more than 9,000 rooms. From the top of this tree, we can see into the Forbidden City. It's not close, but we can see how big it is and see the tops of the buildings. The quarter square mile that is the Forbidden City itself has blocks of buildings and halls and terraces.

Sit on that limb over there and you can see some of the ponds and the river that flows through the Imperial City. The brick courtyards are so huge that a person would look like an ant from where we sit.

My father says the emperor's rooms are behind his throne room in the back of the palace complex. His wife probably has her own set of rooms—maybe her own building. Father said that many of the men and almost all of the women never set foot outside the Forbidden City. They have everything they need inside.

The smaller buildings around the edges are for storage, cooking food, and making whatever the royal family needs. The eunuchs who serve the emperor and his family have living quarters in the palace complex. The eunuchs are special servants and are the only men allowed near the women who live in the Forbidden City. Emperor Wanli has more than one wife, although there is only one empress. She is his first wife. The other women are treated like wives, but they are not officially married to the emperor.[2]

There are maids in the palace complex, but the eunuchs do the real work in the Forbidden

The eunuch Tian Yi was honored with a special tomb, which still stands in modern Bejiing. He served three generations of Ming emperors. The Eunuch Culture Museum has been built around Tian Yi's tomb.

The Chinese are famous for their ceramics. Even servants were depicted in ceramic figures during the Ming Dynasty.

City. Father says there are several hundred eunuchs living and working there. They cook and clean and have many other duties. They can be personal assistants to the empress and the other wives. Some eunuchs take care of the emperor. High-ranking eunuchs can become wealthy.[3]

I don't think I'd like to be one of the emperor's children. I'm sure they have fine clothes and food and many servants to take care of them, but they cannot go outside the city walls. They probably have to do boring things like stand around at ceremonies. Emperor Wanli is still young, but other emperors have had as many as fifty children. The emperor would never pay any attention to you unless you were his first- or second-born son. Father said most royal children are raised by servants. Some royal mothers don't even see their children every day. I wouldn't want to live like that.

Come on, let's go. We've got lots more to see. I'll show you where my father works.

# THE POWERFUL EUNUCHS

Eunuchs served Chinese royal families throughout all of Chinese imperial history, but their power reached its peak during the Ming Dynasty. These special servants worked in the Forbidden City partly because they didn't have families. Since they could not have children of their own, they could devote their attention to their jobs. Often they came from poor families, starting out in menial jobs but hoping to become wealthy while serving the emperor.

There was a hierarchy among the eunuchs, including 24 agencies that supervised such areas as care of utensils, handling of documents and art objects, providing fuel, and music. The highest agency was the Directorate of Ceremonial, whose director was the chief of the palace staff.[4] This director and other high-ranking eunuchs often had great influence over the emperor and his family. Those who served a particular emperor from childhood sometimes became very powerful advisers.[5]

By the late Ming period, eunuch power extended outside the Forbidden City. Sometimes eunuchs became military commanders or tax collectors. They often used extortion and bribery to plump up their own personal treasuries.[6]

In his later years, Wanli withdrew into the Forbidden City Palace. He did not see his officials for months at a time. He only responded to matters of war and finance. His servants controlled all communications that reached him, and they often replied on his behalf. Unofficially, they governed the country, and there was little outside officials could do about it.[7]

The Ming Dynasty had many ineffective emperors. It may have collapsed much earlier had it not been for the work of the eunuchs.

# CHAPTER 4

# Working for the Government

The building Father works in is down this street. His job is in the Ministry of Works where he's in charge of the repair of the Grand Canal. The canal goes all the way from Peking to Nanking. It is the only way to ship grain and other goods to Peking.

Father supervises keeping the canal clear and deep enough. He says that floods bring dirt into the canal from the rivers. If he didn't keep the canal dredged and repaired, ships would drag on the bottom. My father directs the workers who maintain the canal. I'm proud that he has an important job.[1]

When I grow up, I think I would like a job in the Ministry of Works, too. Maybe I'll work in the Great Wall construction and repair division. We can't go see the Great Wall because it is several miles from Peking, but it is a huge, thick wall built to protect China from invasion by the northern tribes. We have to keep it repaired. That's what I

The Great Wall

want to do after I finish my education if I don't become a great scholar.

I go to a school near our home, but I also have a tutor who visits weekly. At school I study reading and counting, and I learn how to write the Chinese symbols. The writing is the hardest part. Each symbol takes several strokes of the brush, with some narrow and some broad. I often use too much ink on my brush and make blots. Then I have to start all over again.

The English word "calligraphy" means "beautiful writing." In China, calligraphy is considered both an everyday practice of writing and an art. Chinese calligraphy is done with a brush and ink.

**Born in 551 BCE, Confucius was a philosopher who taught over 3,000 disciples his ideas about family life, education, and public policy. He advocated strict ethical standards and the practice of educating everyone, rich or poor.**

My tutor comes to teach me the writings of Confucius. Confucius was a great teacher who lived about two thousand years ago. We try to follow all of his teachings. Studying with my tutor will give me a head start on passing my government examinations because they cover Confucius's writings. Later, I may go to an academy or government university to prepare for my tests. It takes many years of study to pass all of the tests, but I'm determined to pass the highest level before I am thirty years old.[2]

The government examinations are given every three years. Tests begin in your own school. If you do well on those tests, you can progress to the county tests and then to the provincial level. That level is very difficult, and many students don't pass. The ones who do pass may then take the higher-level test in Peking or attend an imperial university for more study.

Passing the provincial level test gives a scholar a licentiate degree. Then he can be appointed to a low-level civil service job. If he is able to pass the three-day test in Peking, which gives him a doctoral degree, the emperor will likely give him an important job. My father passed that test. His score was one of the highest, and that's why he has such a good job.[3]

Let's stop here in this park. Sometimes there is a puppet show to watch. Over there is the wagon for the show. I love puppet shows, and I heard that the emperor does, too. I think everyone

Shadow puppet shows are said to have originated in China during the reign of Emperor Wu of the Han Dynasty who ruled from 141 to 87 BCE. Most shadow puppet shows tell war stories or stories of Buddhist monks.

in China must like puppets because they have been around for a long, long time. There are different kinds of puppets, such as stick puppets, with figures glued to thin sticks, and shadow puppets.

The ones I like the best are the ones this show has. They are marionettes with thin strings attached to the hands, feet, head, knees, and other parts of the puppets. Someone stands above the little stage and pulls the strings to make the marionettes move. I don't know how they can handle all those strings at the same time, but I'd like to learn. The shows I like the best are the exciting ones about Zhu Yuanzhang, who conquered the Mongols to become the first Ming emperor.[4]

Let's walk back to my house and I'll tell you more about living here in Peking.

**Chinese marionettes are richly dressed in bright colors.**

# THE GREAT WALL

There is a rumor that the Great Wall of China can be seen from space. This historic monument flows as a river might through the mountains and plains of northern China. In 1929, historian L. Newton Hayes said, "The Great Wall is to China what the pyramids are to the land of the Pharaohs."[5]

The Great Wall began as many smaller walls. Natural barriers protected China on every side except the north. The northern border lay open to raiding nomadic tribes. Before China was unified under one emperor in 221 BCE, many small kingdoms ruled their own areas in a feudal type of government. These kingdoms built walls to protect their lands from the nomads and from one another.

The first emperor, Shih Huang Ti, ordered the walls be connected to provide protection for all. An estimated one million men used packed dirt to build that first connecting piece. Many of them were peasants and criminals who were forced to work away from home for years. Reports from that time say that as the workers died from the harsh conditions, their bodies were thrown into the embankment and covered with more dirt.[6]

There were at least two other major Great Wall projects before the Ming Dynasty started a grand extension of the wall beginning in 1449. Portions of that wall still stand. The Ming used bricks and mortar whenever possible. They placed guard and signal towers along the top. Although the wall blocked invasions from the north for hundreds

The Great Wall of China

of years, it did not stop the Manchus from swarming into China in 1644. They eventually put an end to the Ming Dynasty.[7]

The estimated length of the wall is 5,500 miles (8,800 kilometers), but there are loops, parallel walls, and right-angle spurs that make it difficult to measure. Its width and height vary, but its average height measures 20 feet (6 meters). Its width averages from 25 feet (7.6 meters) at the base to 15 feet (4.5 meters) across the paths on top. Five or six horsemen could ride side by side along these paths.[8]

Is it large enough to see from space? While satellites can zoom in with their cameras, astronauts on the International Space Station admit they cannot see it from there.[9]

# CHAPTER 5
# Temples and Ships

Let's go back to my house. I want to show you something I have there. But on the way we'll pass some places I think you'll like to see.

Over here is a Buddhist temple. This one is small, but there are many large ones in Peking. The Altar of Heaven where we saw Emperor Wanli this morning is one of them. It has many rooms and courtyards. We worship the Buddha here and in the other temples. Our religion, Buddhism, has been around for hundreds of years. Religious scholars, called monks, take care of the temples and hold ceremonies to honor the Buddha.

Do you smell that sweet odor? It comes from the incense that is burning in the temple. Its smoke is an offering to our ancestors who have died. I like the smell,

Chinese Admiral Zheng sailed the world in the 15th century on large wooden ships that were said to be the largest ever built. The dispute was settled in 1962 when a ship rudderpost was found in the ruins of a Ming-period boatyard in Nanking.

Archaeologists calculated that the 36-foot- (11-meter-) long rudderpost must have been built for a ship that was around 500 feet (180 meters) long. This length is longer than the previously estimated 400-foot-long treasure ships of Zheng He.

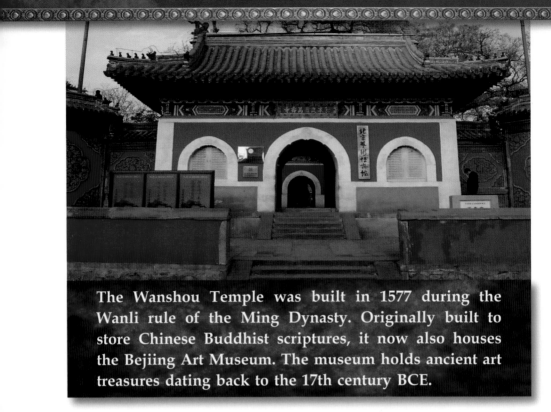

The Wanshou Temple was built in 1577 during the Wanli rule of the Ming Dynasty. Originally built to store Chinese Buddhist scriptures, it now also houses the Bejiing Art Museum. The museum holds ancient art treasures dating back to the 17th century BCE.

but my sister says it makes her stomach hurt. We don't tell our parents about that because they would think it was disrespectful to talk that way about the temple offerings.[1]

The monks chant prayers and meditate for many hours. They help the poor and sick, but the best part is when they hold a festival in the courtyards. There are puppet shows, music, and dancing. The food is good, too.

If my little brothers or I get sick after attending a festival, our parents will call for the physician to come. They are always afraid that we're suffering from a dangerous condition. Usually the physician says that if we didn't eat so many sweets at the festival, we wouldn't get sick. Then he gives our parents a list of herbs to buy. Our mother will boil the herbs in water to make special tea, which we have to drink to make us well. It tastes terrible, but it works.

Here is an herb shop on this corner. All of these little wooden drawers and boxes contain different kinds of dried plants as well as some crushed minerals. The shop owner takes the list the physician has made and measures out small amounts of each herb or mineral. Chinese physicians have gathered plants since ancient days. They test them to see if they will cure sicknesses.

Sometimes physicians use acupuncture to treat illness. Once I had a very high fever after I fell and cut my leg. It was a small cut, but it got red and my leg swelled. The physician gave me herbal tea, then he put some very thin needles under my skin in different places to adjust my ch'i, or life energy flow. I was afraid because the needles were long, but it didn't hurt, and I was better the next day. I'm not sure how acupuncture works, but that's something else I'm going to study someday.[2]

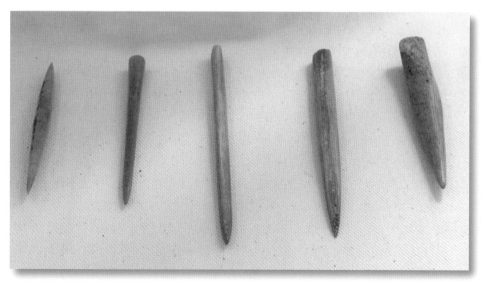

Early acupuncture needles were sometimes made of bone or stone. The bone ones above were likely just pressed against the skin at certain points rather than inserted. Later needles were made of gold, silver, bronze, and bamboo. They were thin enough to be inserted into the skin.

This model of one of Admiral Zheng He's famous treasure ships shows the nine bamboo sails that powered the huge ship. It took many seamen to handle the sails, but the numerous sails allowed the ship to travel fast in spite of a heavy cargo load.

Here's my house again. I want to show you something in my room. It's a model of one of Admiral Zheng He's ships. Zheng He led a great fleet on seven voyages to distant countries. Emperor Zhu Di of the Yongle reign wanted to send ships to visit and trade with other countries, and he chose Zheng He to be in charge.

In 1405, Zheng He set off on his first voyage. Sixty of his 317 ships were huge—as long as 400 feet (120 meters) and as wide as 165 feet (50 meters). The big ships carried tons of Chinese products like porcelain vases and silk fabrics. They were often called treasure ships. At each seaport the fleet would stop to trade for that country's treasures. The rest of the ships were smaller. They were used to protect the treasure ships and carry supplies.

The big ships had as many as nine woven bamboo sails with dozens of cabins and holds to carry soldiers, merchants, sailors, physicians, astrologers, and many other workers. The items used for trade were stacked in big holds below deck.

Zheng He had many adventures as he traveled along the Southern Chinese coast and around the Indonesian Islands. He sailed to India and Arabia and finally to the east coast of Africa. Sometimes he and his soldiers stopped along the way to fight pirates and rescue kings. He brought back all sorts of animals and treasures to the emperor, and he often brought visitors as well. Sometimes the visitors stayed in Peking for a couple years before Zheng He could take them home again.[3]

Statue of Zheng He

I like ships, so if I can't pass my exams, I may go to Nanjing where they build ships. They aren't as grand as Zheng He's, but I think I could also be an adventurer like him. I don't think my parents would like that choice, but it would be exciting to sail to foreign lands. Don't you agree?

I see that you must leave. I'm sorry you have to go because there's more to see in Peking. But I do have to do my chores before our evening meal. I'm supposed to feed the fish in the pond and weed our herb garden. I also think my grandmother wants me to go to the shops to buy more thread for her embroidery. By the time I do all of that, I will have to clean up for our meal.

After we eat, my mother will send me to bed because I have to get up early tomorrow for school. I hope you'll come again. Then maybe my older brother will go with us to see the Great Wall. We can run a race on top of the wall, if the soldiers aren't watching. Wouldn't that be fun?

# China's Great Admiral

Zheng He was born in the southern province of Yunnan. His family was on the Mongols' side when Chinese rebels began fighting. When the Mongols lost, Zheng He's father was killed. The boy, who was just ten or eleven years old, was taken prisoner.

Zheng He became a servant in the palace. He served in the court of Zhu Di, who would become the Yongle emperor. Zheng He was ambitious and smart and soon became indispensable. When Zhu Di came to power, Zheng He was right by his side as a valued adviser.[4]

The Yongle emperor decided to send a great fleet of ships to visit other countries, and he chose Zheng He to be in charge. The purpose of the trip wasn't to explore new lands, but to ask other countries to cooperate with the new emperor. Called the tribute system, this was actually a way to inform other countries that China was boss and they should send gifts to the emperor to show that they understood.[5]

Although he had no experience with ships or the sea, Zheng He was an expert organizer. His giant fleet set out from Nanking with at least 28,000 men. They brought back tons of exotic goods from lands as far away as Africa.

The great admiral died on the return trip of his seventh voyage and was buried at sea. A new emperor commanded that all shipbuilding cease. He wanted China to forget the rest of the world, so he ordered no more voyages. China was turning toward isolation, leaving Zheng He to be the only famous admiral of Imperial China.[6]

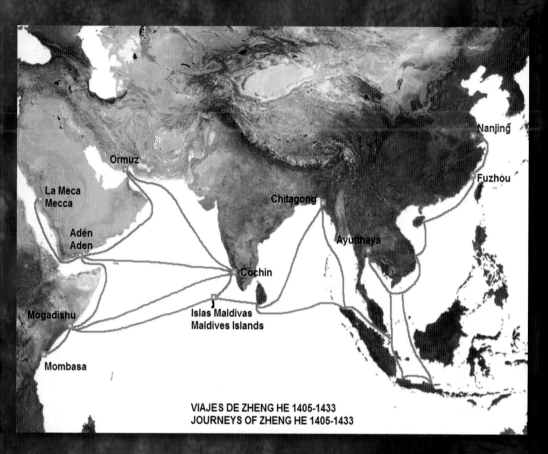

VIAJES DE ZHENG HE 1405-1433
JOURNEYS OF ZHENG HE 1405-1433

Admiral Zheng He's fleet crisscrossed the seas of southern Asia during seven voyages between 1405 and 1433. The ships traveled as far west as Mombasa on the eastern coast of Africa and Mecca in Arabia, which is in present-day Saudi Arabia.

**BCE**

**221**      First Emperor unifies China.

**220**      Construction of the Great Wall begins.

**CE**

**68**       First Buddhist Temple in China is founded.

**105**      First paper is made by Cai Lun.

**589**      First historical reference to toilet paper is made.

**610**      The Grand Canal is finished.

**1088**     The compass is first described in a book.

**1206**     Genghis Khan founds Mongol Empire.

**1271**     Kublai Khan, grandson of Genghis, founds Yuan Dynasty.

**1368**     The Yuan Dynasty is overthrown by Zhu Yuanzhang, who founds the Ming Dynasty.

**1403**     Zhu Di becomes Yongle Emperor.

**1405**     Zheng He takes his first voyage.

**1406**     Construction of the Forbidden City begins.

**1420**     Peking (Beijing) becomes the new capital of China.

**1556**     The Shaanxi earthquake kills 850,000 people.

**1572**     Emperor Wanli's reign begins.

**1582**     Jesuits begin mission work in China.

**1644**     The Qing Dynasty is established after the Ming Dynasty is defeated by the Manchus.

**1911**     Revolution ends the period of Imperial China.

**1912**     Sun Yat-sen becomes the first president of the Republic of China.

**1949**     The People's Republic of China is founded under Mao Zedong

**1970s**    Chinese method of translation is changed. Peking is then pronounced as "Beijing."

**Chapter One. Welcome to Peking**

1. Ray Huang, *1587: A Year of No Significance: The Ming Dynasty in Decline* (New Haven and London: Yale University Press, 1981), pp. 118–119.
2. Albert Chan, *The Glory and Fall of the Ming Dynasty* (Norman: University of Oklahoma Press, 1982), p. 95.
3. Timothy Brook, *The Confusions of Pleasure: Commerce and Culture in Ming China* (Berkeley: University of California Press, 1998), p. 154.
4. China Highlights, "The Yuan Dynasty," © 1998, http://www.chinahighlights.com/travelguide/ china-history/the-yuan-dynasty.htm
5. *Mongolia,* "The Yuan Dynasty," U.S. Library of Congress, http://countrystudies.us/mongolia/ 19.htm
6. Carrie Gracie, "Kublai Khan: China's Favourite Barbarian," *BBC News Magazine,* October 8, 2012, http://www.bbc.co.uk/news/magazine-19850234

**Chapter Two. My Home in the *Hutong***

1. Hao Zhuo, "*Hutong* and *Siheyuan* in Beijing," http://chineseculture.about.com/library/weekly/ aa020501a.htm
2. Skwirk.com, "Daily Life of Women," http://www.skwirk.com.au/p-c_s-14_u-173_t-472_c-1711/ act/history/ancient-societies-china/ancient-china-part-ii/daily-life-of-women-
3. Patricia Buckley Ebrey, "Homes: Kang," *A Visual Sourcebook of Chinese Civilization,* http://depts. washington.edu/chinaciv/home/3hkang.htm
4. Ibid.
5. Destiny: The Culture of China, "Traditional Music," http://library.thinkquest.org/20443/ traditional_music.html
6. China Culture, "Costume in the Ming Dynasty," http://www1.chinaculture.org/ library/2008-01/28/content_28364.htm
7. China Information Internet Center, "Imperial Food in the Ming Dynasty," http://www.china. org.cn/english/imperial/26109.htm
8. Destiny: The Culture of China, "Food and Drink," http://library.thinkquest.org/20443/g_food_ drink.html
9. China Information Internet Center, "Imperial Food in the Ming Dynasty," http://www.china. org.cn/english/imperial/26109.htm.

**Chapter Three. The Forbidden City**

1. Ray Huang, *1587: A Year of No Significance: The Ming Dynasty in Decline* (New Haven and London: Yale University Press, 1981), pp. 12–13.
2. Irving Hultengren, "Concubines," http://www.mingtombs.eu/o/cocu/cocu.html
3. Charles O. Hucker, *The Ming Dynasty: Its Origins and Evolving Institutions* (Ann Arbor: Center for Chinese Studies, The University of Michigan, 1978), pp. 93–94.
4. Charles O. Hucker, *The Traditional Chinese State in Ming Times* (1368–1644) (Tucson: The University of Arizona Press, 1961), p. 94.
5. Hucker, p. 92.

6. Jeffrey Hays, "Facts and Details: Eunuchs in China," 2008, http://factsanddetails.com/china.php?itemid=43

7. John W. Dardess, *Ming China,* 1368–1644 (Lanham, MD: Rowman & Littlefield Publishers, Inc., 2012) p. 54.

**Chapter Four. Working for the Government**

1. Timothy Brook, *The Confusions of Pleasure: Commerce and Culture in Ming China* (Berkeley: University of California Press, 1998), pp. 46–49.

2. Destiny: The Culture of China. "Philosophy," http://library.thinkquest.org/20443/g_philosophy.html

3. Charles O. Hucker, *The Traditional Chinese State in Ming Times* (1368–1644) (Tucson: The University of Arizona Press, 1961), pp. 14–17.

4. Destiny: The Culture of China, "Puppetry," http://library.thinkquest.org/20443/g_puppetry.html

5. L. Newton Hayes, *The Great Wall of China* (Shanghai: Kelly & Walsh, Ltd, 1929), p. 2.

6. Hayes, pp. 41–42.

7. Great Wall of China, "Great Wall History," 2009, http://www.greatwall-of-china.com/51-90/the-great-wall-of-china.html

8. Hayes, p. 50.

9. "China's Wall Less Great in View from Space," NASA, May 9, 2005, http://www.nasa.gov/vision/space/workinginspace/great_wall.html

**Chapter Five. Temples and Ships**

1. Margaret Kelly, Editor, *Fodor's China,* 7th Edition (New York: Fodor's Travel, 2011) pp. 348–351.

2. Destiny: The Culture of China, "Medicine," http://library.thinkquest.org/20443/g_medicine.html

3. Michael Yamishita, *Zhenghe: Tracing the Epic Voyages of China's Greatest Explorer* (Vercelli, Italy: White Star Publishers, 2006) pp. 32–35.

4. Yamishita, pp. 22–24.

5. Robert Finlay, "The Voyages of Zheng He: Ideology, State Power, and Maritime Trade in Ming China," *The Journal of the Historical Society,* VII:3, September 3, 2008.

6. Yamishita, pp. 35, 44–46.

**Books**

Cotterell, Arthur, photos by Alan Hill and Geoff Brightling. *Eyewitness: Ancient China.* New York: DK Publishing, Inc., 2005.

Morley, Jacqueline, illustrations by David Antram. *You Wouldn't Want to Work on the Great Wall of China! Defenses You'd Rather Not Build.* New York: Franklin Watts, 2006.

Platt, Richard; illustrations by Manuela Cappon. *Through Time: Beijing; Great Dynasties, Mighty Conflicts . . . and the Forbidden City.* New York: Kingfisher, 2008.

Webster, Christine. *Structural Wonders: Great Wall of China.* New York: Weigl Publishers, Inc., 2008.


**Works Consulted**

Brook, Timothy. *The Confusions of Pleasure; Commerce and Culture in Ming China.* Berkeley: University of California Press, 1998.

Chan, Albert. *The Glory and Fall of the Ming Dynasty.* Norman: University of Oklahoma Press, 1982.

Chang, Yu-Chuan. *Studies in Chinese History and Civilization: Wang Shou-Jen as a Statesman.* Peking: The Chinese Social & Political Science Association, 1940. Reprinted in 1975 by University Publications of America, Inc.

China Culture. "Costume in the Ming Dynasty," http://www1.chinaculture.org/library/2008-01/28/content_28364.htm

China Highlights. http://www.chinahighlights.com/travelguide/china-history/the-yuan-dynasty.htm

China Information Internet Center. "Imperial Food in the Ming Dynasty," http://www.china.org.cn/english/imperial/26109.htm

Dardess, John W. *Ming China, 1368–1644.* Lanham, MD: Rowman & Littlefield Publishers, Inc., 2012.

———. *A Ming Society: T'ai-ho County, Kiangsi, Fourteenth to Seventeenth Centuries.* Berkeley: University of California Press, 1996.

*Destiny: The Culture of China.* http://library.thinkquest.org/20443/g_philosophy.html

Ebrey, Patricia Buckley. *Confucianism and Family Rituals in Imperial China.* Princeton: Princeton University Press, 1991.

———. *A Visual Sourcebook of Chinese Civilization.* http://depts.washington.edu/chinaciv/

Finlay, Robert. "The Voyages of Zheng He: Ideology, State Power, and Maritime Trade in Ming China," *The Journal of the Historical Society,* VIII:3, September 2008.

Gracie, Carrie. "Kublai Khan: China's Favorite Barbarian," *BBC News Magazine,* October 8, 2012. http://www.bbc.co.uk/news/magazine-19850234

*Great Wall of China.* "Great Wall History." 2009. http://www.greatwall-of-china.com/51-90/the-great-wall-of-china.html

Hadingham, Evan. "Nova: Ancient Chinese Explorers." PBS. www.pbs.org/wgbh/nova/ancient/ancient-chinese-explorers.html

Hayes, L. Newton. *The Great Wall of China.* Shanghai: Kelly & Walsh, Ltd, 1929.

Hays, Jeffrey. *China: Facts & Details.* 2008. http://factsanddetails.com/china.php

Huang, Ray. *1587: A Year of No Significance: The Ming Dynasty in Decline.* New Haven and London: Yale University Press, 1981.

Hucker, Charles O. *The Ming Dynasty: Its Origins and Evolving Institutions.* Ann Arbor: Center for Chinese Studies, The University of Michigan, 1978.

———. *The Traditional Chinese State in Ming Times (1368–1644).* Tucson: The University of Arizona Press, 1961.

Kelly, Margaret, editor. *Fodor's China, 7th Edition.* New York: Fodor's Travel, 2011.

Ming Tombs Special Administration, Beijing. http://www.mingtombs.com/e_home/

Mongolia, "The Yuan Dynasty," http://countrystudies.us/mongolia/19.htm

Mote, Frederick W., and Denis Twitchett, editors. *The Cambridge History of China, Volume 7, The Ming Dynasty, 1368-1644,* Part 1. Cambridge, UK: Cambridge University Press, 1988.

Oakland Museum of California. "Secret World of the Forbidden City." 1999. http://museumca.org/exhibit/exhib_fc2.html

Skwirk.com. "Daily Life of Women." http://www.skwirk.com.au/p-c_s-14_u-173_t-472_c-1711/act/history/ancient-societies-china/ancient-china-part-ii/daily-life-of-women-

Yamashita, Michael. *Zhenghe: Tracing the Epic Voyages of China's Greatest Explorer.* Vercelli, Italy: White Star Publishers, 2006.

Zhuo, Hao. "*Hutong* and *Siheyuan* in Beijing." http://chineseculture.about.com/library/weekly/aa020501a.htm

**On the Internet**

Ducksters, "Explorers for Kids: Zheng He"
http://www.ducksters.com/biography/explorers/zheng_he.php

National Geographic Kids, "China Facts and Pictures"
http://kids.nationalgeographic.com/kids/claces/find/china

Taylor, Amie. "Facts About the Great Wall of China for Kids," *USA Today.*
http://traveltips.usatoday.com/great-wall-china-kids-61571.html

**abacus**—A simple adding machine that has beads that slide along rods.

**academy**—A private school.

**barbarian**—A person in a culture that is believed to be savage, primitive, or uncivilized.

**cape**—A coat without sleeves that hangs loosely over the shoulders and back.

**chant**—To sing a song on the same note or same few notes throughout.

**civil service**—Any branch of government that is not part of the courts, military, or a religious organization.

**courtyard**—An open space surrounded by buildings or walls.

**custom**—A way of acting that is usual or accepted for a person or social group.

**dredge**—To remove dirt from the bottom of a body of water.

**drought**—A long period of time with little or no rain.

**embankment**—A mound of dirt piled high.

**embroidery**—The art or result of sewing designs on cloth.

**empress**—The official wife of an emperor.

**exotic**—Unusual and interesting items or people from a foreign place.

**extortion**—The act of using power or threats to gain money or information.

**famine**—A great lack of food over a wide area.

**feudal**—A system of lords and vassals who work for the lord in return for the lord's protection.

**fleet**—A group of ships under one commander.

**incense**—A powdery substance that has a strong odor when burned.

**isolation**—Set apart or separate so as to be alone.

**jade**—A hard green stone or the color of that stone.

**kowtow**—To bow so low that the face touches the ground; a sign of submission.

**licentiate**—A degree that awards a license and is just below a doctorate.

**meditate**—To think calmly, deeply, and at length on an idea or subject.

**menial**—Lowly or simple.

**natural barriers**—Any type of land formation or body of water that may serve as protection.

**nomadic**—Having no set home; moving from place to place according to opportunity.

**peasant**—A member of a class of farm workers.

**physician**—A doctor.

**porcelain**—A type of white, shiny pottery.

**procession**—A line or group of people moving forward in a formal, orderly way.

**provincial**—Dealing with a province, a governmental area that contains several counties.

**rudderpost**—A long wooden oar-like device that is used to steer a ship.

**sedan chair**—An enclosed box on poles in which important people may sit so as to be carried by servants.

**self-sufficient**—Able to survive without help from others.

**stabilize**—To make firm or steady.

**tribute**—Something given to express respect.

**tunic**—A long shirt that hangs down below the waist.